Earring Box

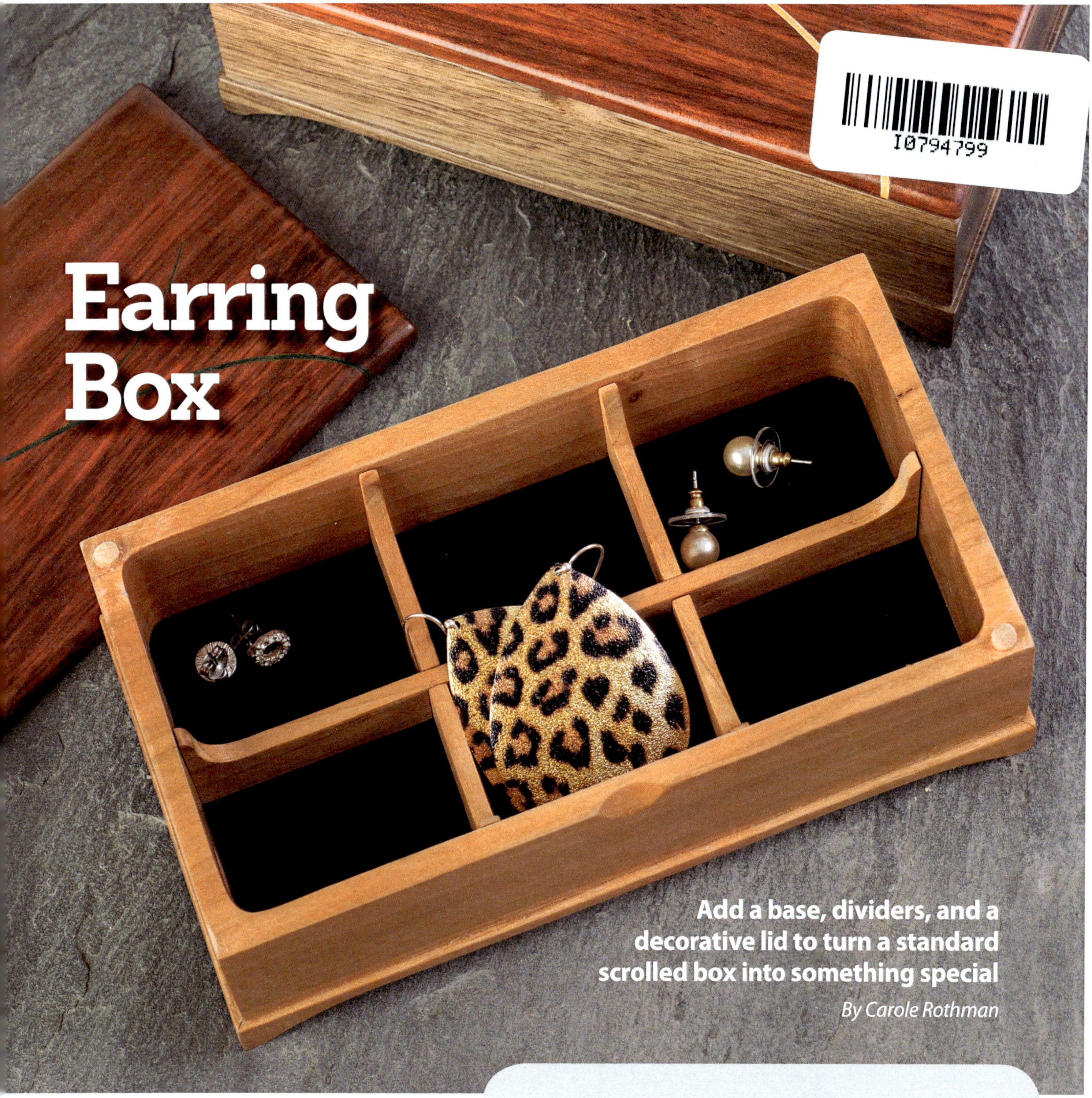

Add a base, dividers, and a decorative lid to turn a standard scrolled box into something special

By Carole Rothman

Although the expression "good things come in small packages" usually refers to the gift, not its box, this graceful project is both a small package and a gift. Designed to mimic conventional box construction, it takes full advantage of the scroll saw's capacity for both internal and compound cuts. The decorative lid, held in place by small dowels, features crosscut veneer, while the egg-crate divider carries the curved theme to the velvet-lined interior of the box.

Working with Veneer

I strongly recommend that you use cyanoacrylate (CA) glue formulated for wood when gluing the veneer into place, because clamping would be difficult and a quick set time is needed. If you find it challenging to get a tight joint with three layers of veneer, use one or two layers instead. If you don't want to use CA glue, attach a single layer of veneer with a wood glue with a short open time, like Weldbond or Titebond Quick & Thick. However, because of the longer set time, these glues require several minutes of hand clamping to ensure a good bond. Regardless of the number of strips or type of adhesive, practice with scrap wood and veneer before gluing the actual lid.

MAKING THE BODY

1 **Attach the box body pattern to the blank.** Use an awl to mark the drilling points for the dowel holes and the blade-entry hole. Drill the blade-entry hole, insert a #5 premium blade, cut along the inner line, and then cut along the outer line. Mark the front with a pencil and remove the pattern.

2 **Drill the dowel holes.** Use a $\frac{3}{16}$" (5mm)-diameter bit and make each hole ½" (13mm) deep. Glue dowels into the holes, pressing firmly to seat them.

3 **Round the inside corners.** Use a spindle sander to remove burn and blade marks. Be careful not to add gouges. You will sand the box body further in Step 9.

MAKING THE LID

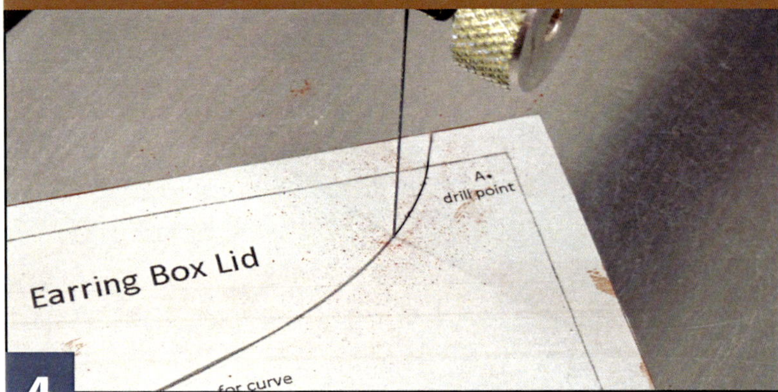

4 **Choose the most attractive orientation of the lid blank for the top and front of the lid.** Mark this position lightly with a pencil. Place the wood *facedown* and attach a copy of the lid pattern to the *underside.* Align the front of the pattern with the front edge of the lid. Cut smoothly along the curved line with a #3 reverse-tooth blade. Remove the pattern.

5 **Apply the veneer.** Place the two lid pieces *face up* on a flat surface covered with waxed paper or a nonstick mat. Apply cyanoacrylate (CA) glue formulated for wood to the curved edge of one lid piece and spread it evenly with a toothpick. Use your fingers to press a white veneer strip firmly into place along the glued edge. Make sure the bottom surface of the lid piece and the veneer are flush and that the outer surface of the veneer is free of glue. Press the other lid piece briefly against the veneer to exert firm pressure. When the white veneer is secure, attach the yellow veneer using the same method. Repeat the process for the final white strip. Then, attach the other lid piece, making sure that the bottom faces are flush. Hold the pieces firmly together until the glue sets. When it's fully dry, sand both faces until smooth. The lid should end up around $\frac{5}{16}$" (8mm) thick.

6 **Attach a second copy of the lid pattern to the underside of the lid.** Match the curve in the pattern to the one in the lid. Mark the dowel drill points with an awl and drill 3/16" (5mm)-diameter by 3/16" (5mm)-deep holes. If you are using a brad-point bit, be sure that the point does not penetrate the face of the lid. Cut to the outside of the lid perimeter line. Remove the pattern.

7 **Place the lid on the box body.** Sand the dowels and holes just until the lid can be placed and removed easily. With the lid in place, use a belt sander and miter gauge to sand the assembly until the piece is smooth and square, and the sides and lid are flush.

8 **Measure and mark the center of the top edge of the box body front.** Transfer this mark down the front. Set the spindle sander table level and install a 5/8" (16mm)-diameter spindle. Hold the front face of the box body against the spindle at a 30° angle. Sand a small indentation into the front face. Soften it by hand sanding. This indentation allows for easy removal of the lid.

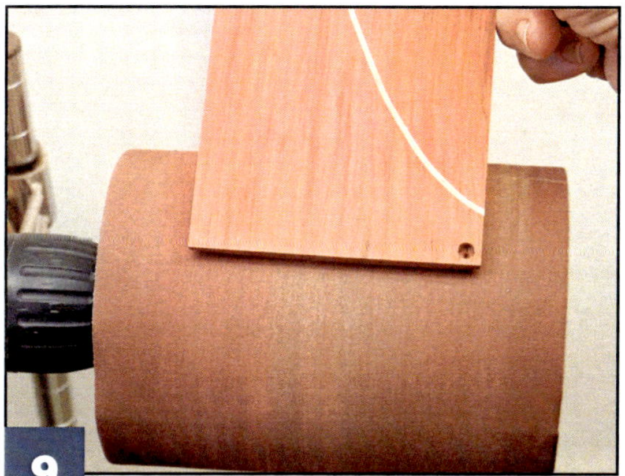

9 **Round the upper edge of the lid.** Use a pneumatic sanding drum. Sand the entire lid to 240 grit, softening the lower edge by hand. Use a detail sander to remove any remaining blade, burn, and sanding marks from the box body and to sand it to 240 grit.

MAKING THE BASE

10 **Place the box body on the box bottom blank.** Trace the inside of the box body and cut it with a #3 blade. Mark the front and upper face of the piece and set it aside.

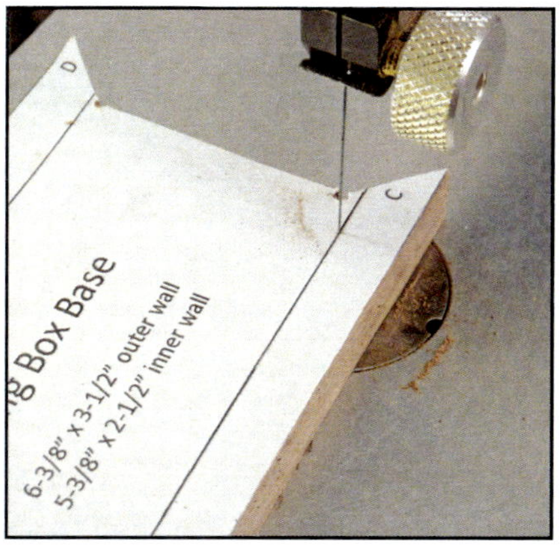

11 **Attach the base pattern to the base blank.** Cut along the outer lines with a #3 blade. Drill blade-entry holes in each of the four corners and use them to cut along the diagonal lines to the outer edge of the base blank. (Cutting from the inside out helps ensure neat diagonal cuts.) Then, cut along the inner lines to separate the pieces. Remove the pattern and transfer the letters from the pattern to the tops of the corresponding pieces.

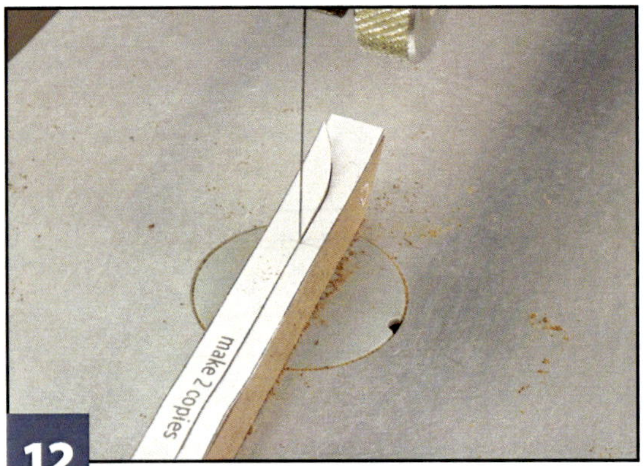

12 **Attach a side pattern to the outer face of each base piece.** Rotate each piece so the pattern faces up, and cut along the lower curve. Remove the pattern. Dry-assemble the base, using the letters to keep the pieces oriented correctly.

13 **Apply glue to the mitered corners and assemble the base.** Use a rubber band to clamp the assembly. (A helper might be useful.) Remove any glue squeeze-out, make sure that the pieces lie flat, and let the assembly dry thoroughly. When dry, sand the upper surface on a sandpaper-covered flat tile to ensure that it is flat and to remove any glue residue.

14 **Center the box body on the base.** The wood that extends beyond the box sides (called the reveal) should be even the whole way around the box. Lightly mark the position of the box body. Then, glue and clamp the box body to the base. Remove any squeeze-out. Then, use sandpaper to soften the top edges of the box and base, and the outer curved edges of the base.

15 **Attach the divider patterns to the blanks.** Cut along the lines, but cut each piece slightly long so you can sand it to fit. Place the plywood bottom cut in Step 10 into the box. *Do not glue it in place.* Insert the long divider to check the length, and sand the ends, if needed, until it slides into place. Repeat for the short dividers. Assemble the unit to check the fit of the mating pieces. Sand the slots if needed. All of the divider pieces should fit snugly without forcing. Sand the divider pieces to 240 grit.

COMPLETING THE PROJECT

16 **Place a drop of glue where the long and short dividers will join.** Slide the short pieces into place, making sure that they are at right angles to the long piece. When dry, place the unit into the box to check its fit, and sand as needed. Remove the dividers and the plywood bottom.

17 **Place the lid on the box, check the fit, and sand as needed.** Remove any sanding dust and apply a sealer coat of shellac to all surfaces of the box, lid, and dividers; allow it to dry. When possible, I use spray shellac, but if you must brush it on, make a 2-pound cut of dewaxed super blonde flakes. Sand with 320-grit sandpaper. Apply several coats of clear spray lacquer to the box and lid, rubbing between coats with 0000 steel wool as needed.

18 **Remove the backing from the velvet.** Position it sticky side up on a self-healing mat. Place the plywood bottom facedown on the adhesive and press firmly. Use a razor knife or cutting wheel to cut the perimeter. Apply a small amount of glue to the underside of the plywood where it will meet the compound-cut base. Press the piece, velvet side up, firmly into place, and insert the dividers.

Materials & Tools

Materials

- Walnut, $1\frac{3}{8}$" (3.5cm) thick: box body, 4" x 7" (10.2cm x 17.8cm)
- Redheart, $\frac{3}{8}$" (1cm) thick: lid, 4" x 7" (10.2cm x 17.8cm)
- Yellow veneer, cut across the grain: $\frac{3}{8}$" x 7" (1cm x 17.8cm)
- White veneer, cut across the grain: 2 each, $\frac{3}{8}$" x 7" (1cm x 17.8cm)
- Baltic birch plywood, $\frac{1}{8}$" (3mm) thick: box bottom, $3\frac{1}{2}$" x $6\frac{1}{2}$" (8.9cm x 16.5cm)
- Walnut, $\frac{1}{2}$" (1.3cm) thick: base, 4" x 7" (10.2cm x 17.8cm)
- Walnut, $\frac{1}{8}$" (3mm) thick: $1\frac{1}{2}$" x $6\frac{1}{2}$" (3.8cm x 16.5cm); 2 each $1\frac{1}{2}$" x $3\frac{1}{2}$" (3.8cm x 8.9cm)
- Dowels, $\frac{3}{16}$" (5mm) dia.: 2 each $\frac{11}{16}$" (1.8cm) long
- Sandpaper
- Glue: wood, cyanoacrylate (CA) glue formulated for wood, such as Dap RapidFuse or Titebond Instant Bond medium or thick
- Waxed paper or nonstick silicone mat
- Self-adhesive velvet: 4" x 7" (10.2cm x 17.8cm)
- Shellac: spray or 2-pound cut dewaxed super blonde flakes
- Lacquer: clear spray
- Steel wool: 0000 grit

Tools

- Scroll saw blades: #5 premium, such as FD Polar; #3 reverse-tooth
- Drill with bit: $\frac{3}{16}$" (5mm) dia.
- Spindle sander with assorted sizes of spindles
- Detail sander with assorted grits of sandpaper
- Belt sander
- Pneumatic drum with 240-grit sleeve
- Awl
- Small clamps: 8 each
- Razor knife or cutting wheel
- Self-healing mat
- Large rubber band (for clamping base)

The author used these products for the project. Substitute your choice of brands, tools, and materials as desired.

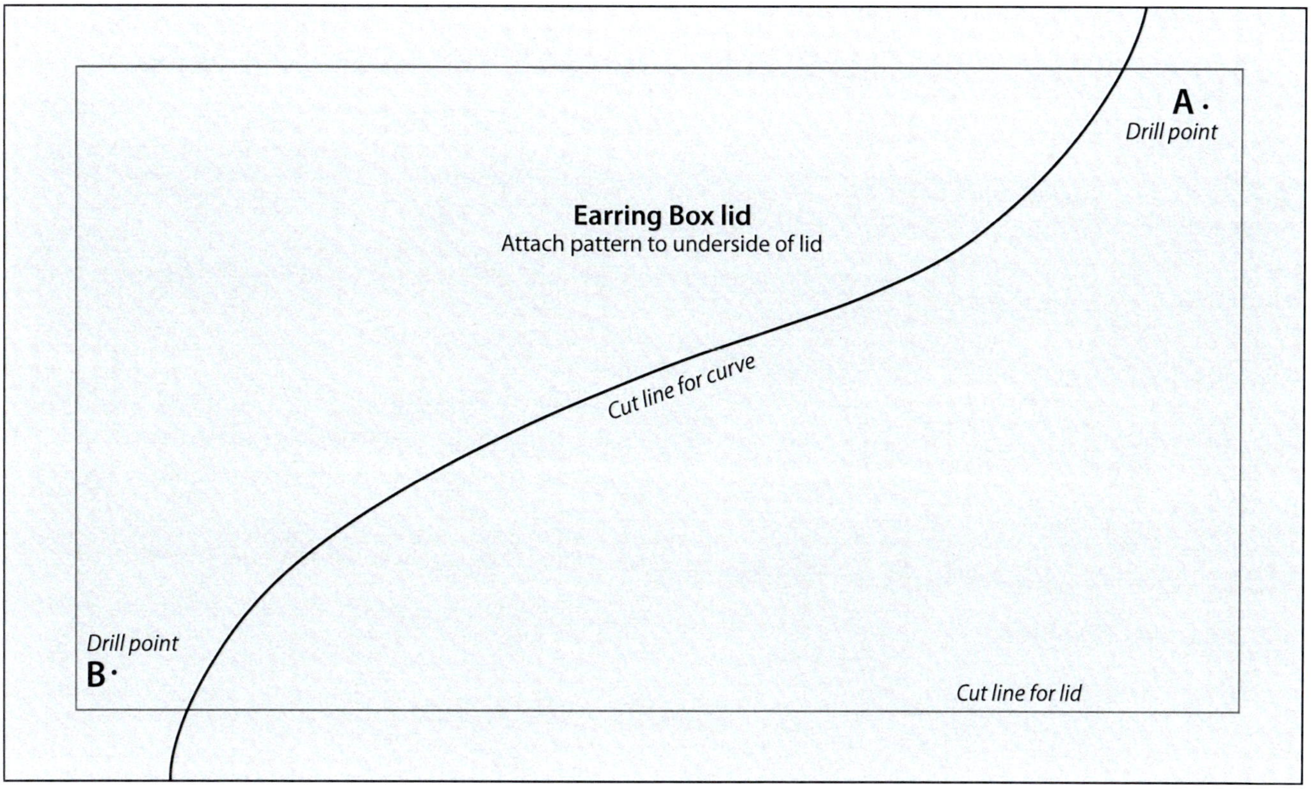

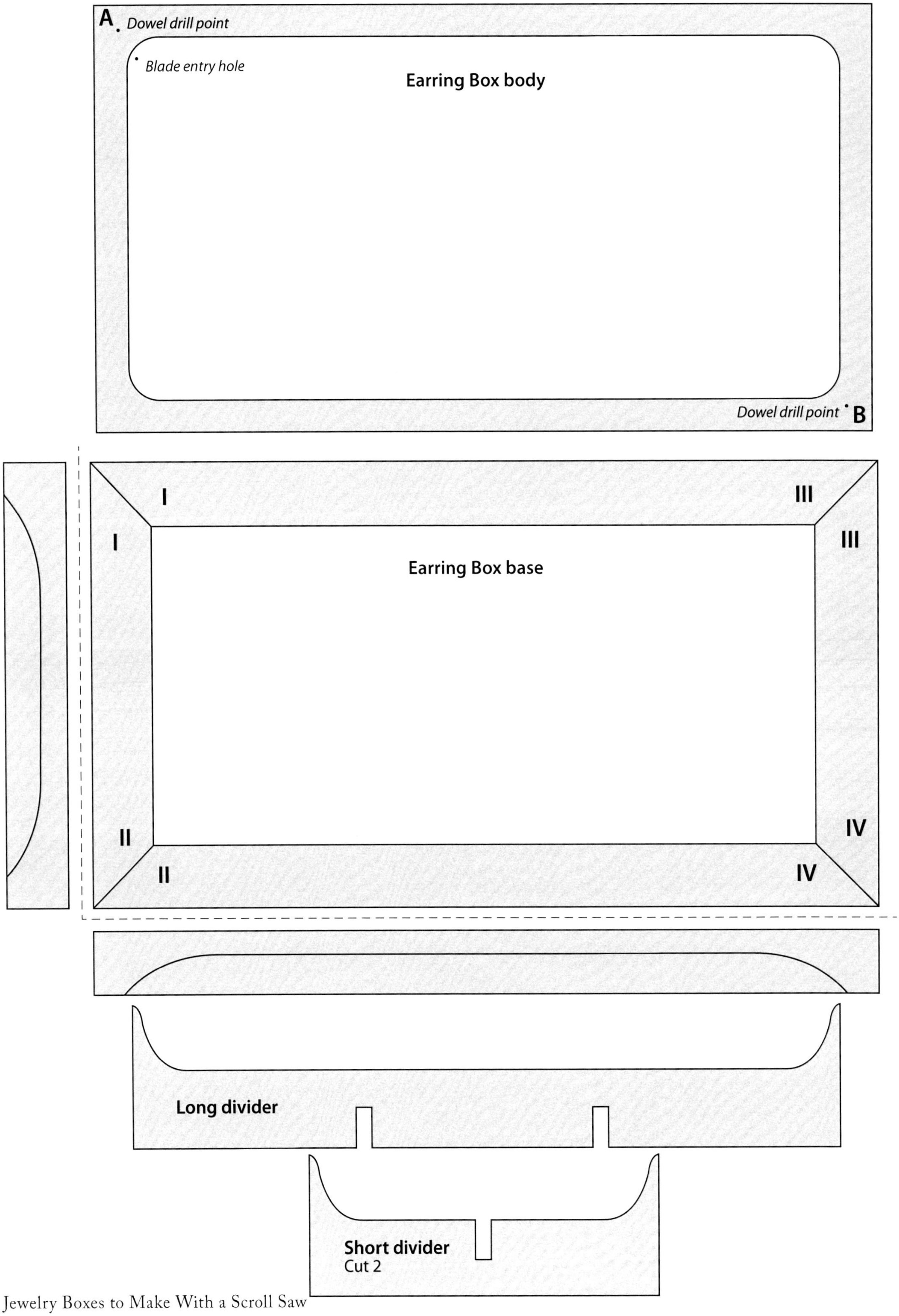
A
Dowel drill point
Blade entry hole
Earring Box body
Dowel drill point
B
I
I
III
III
Earring Box base
II
II
IV
IV
Long divider
Short divider
Cut 2

Making a Maze-Lid Box

Adding a game to the lid makes this box fun as well as functional

By Carole Rothman

The story of this box is like a maze itself, with many paths and a few dead ends before I reached the finish. It started with a search for interesting new box lids. A friend remarked that one of my designs looked like a maze and suggested that an actual maze would make a really neat box lid. Challenged, I found a website that showed how to construct mazes.

Armed with this knowledge and some ¼" graph paper, I got to work. Several versions later, I had my design. To find the right size of ball bearings, I test-drove small sugar balls (dragées, from my cake-decorating days) through the paths.

All that remained was the clear acrylic plastic cover, a material I hadn't used before. After one or two meltdowns, I found the blade (a Flying Dutchman Polar blade) and technique (slow speed) to use. Four small screws later, the maze lid was good to go.

Start by cutting the blanks to the rough sizes listed. Attach the patterns to the blanks using repositionable spray adhesive, and drill the holes marked on the patterns. When drilling the blade-entry holes for the maze area, make sure you center the drill bit between the cutting lines.

CUTTING THE MAZE

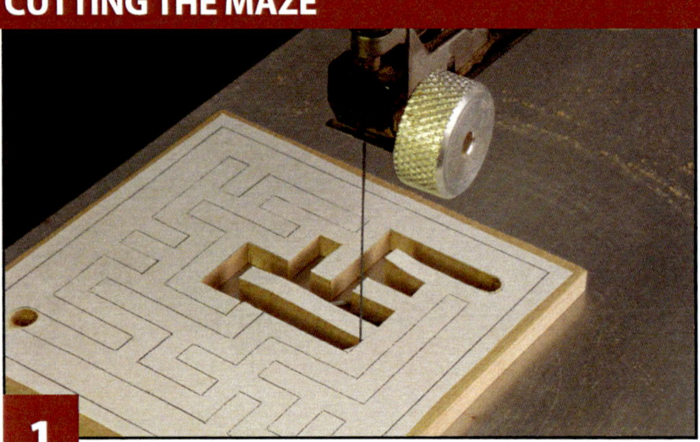

1 **Cut the maze.** Use a #3 blade. Be careful not to break off any of the arms of the maze. Do not cut the outer profile of the lid yet. Cut or tear away the center of the pattern so you can clearly see the cut edges of the maze.

2 **Refine the arms of the maze.** Carefully trim off any cutting irregularities. Gently sand the bottom edges of the arms to remove any "fuzzies." The top edges will be sanded and softened in Step 5. Do not remove the remainder of the pattern yet.

3 **Align the grain directions of the lid middle and lid bottom.** Then, glue and clamp the lid middle to the lid bottom. I used a shop-made bowl press to clamp the small pieces together. Allow the glue to dry, and sand the surface of the lid middle smooth.

4 **Glue the maze elements together.** Align the grain direction of the maze with that of the assembled middle and bottom. Carefully apply dots of glue to the centers of the arms and perimeter using a toothpick. Clamp the pieces together for about five minutes, and then remove the clamps and clean any squeeze-out. Re-clamp the pieces until the glue is fully dry.

5 **Cut just outside the perimeter of the lid.** Cutting the lid slightly large gives you a little extra wood for sanding the sides smooth. Remove the pattern. Carefully soften the edges of the arms of the maze by hand sanding or using a 240-grit mop sander. Sand the outside of the lid lightly to remove blade marks and irregularities; you will do a final sanding of the lid sides in Step 10.

MAKING THE BOX

6 **Cut the box sides.** Attach the pattern to the blank and drill the blade-entry hole. Insert a #9 blade through the entry hole and cut along the inside line to cut away the center of the box. Cut to each corner, back the blade up a bit, and then cut a curve to the next line. Once you remove the center, go back and cut into each corner to free the remaining wood scrap and produce a sharp corner.

7 **Refine the inside of the box.** Sand the inner faces of the box until they are smooth, either by hand or with a detail sander. Do not remove the pattern. Invert the box body on the lid liner blank. Trace the inside of the box onto the blank. Cut along this line to form the lid liner. Sand the edges lightly.

8 **Finish cutting the box.** Align the grain directions of the sides and bottom. Glue and clamp the box bottom to the box sides. Allow the glue to set for five minutes, and then remove the clamps to clean up any glue squeeze-out. Reclamp the box and let the glue dry. Then, cut along the outer perimeter of the box. Sand the sides to remove the blade marks and any large irregularities.

9 **Attach the lid liner.** Invert the lid. Center the lid liner on the lid, and invert the box on top of the lid to position the liner properly. Remove the box carefully and lightly mark the location of the liner with a pencil. Glue and clamp the liner to the lid, using the pencil marks as guides and being careful not to let it slip out of position. Clean up any glue squeeze-out. Let the glue dry thoroughly.

FINISHING THE BOX

10 **Finish the box.** Place the lid on the box, making sure the grains run in the same direction. Clamp the box carefully in a vise. Sand the box and lid to match, using progressively finer grits of sandpaper up to 320 grit.

11 **Apply the finish.** Apply several coats of a clear finish, such as lacquer, to the box and the lid. Be careful to avoid sags or puddles in the maze area. Buff the finish between coats with 0000 steel wool as needed. Remove any dust or particles with a vacuum, moist cloth, or paper towel.

FINISHING THE BOX

12 **Make the pattern for the acrylic top piece.** Place the lid face down on a piece of paper and trace its perimeter. Mark the lid and pattern so you can align the acrylic top properly. Make a mark 3⁄16" (5mm) in from both sides in each corner for the screw pilot holes. This method ensures the lid will fit the maze exactly.

13 **Cut the acrylic.** Attach the pattern to the protective film on the acrylic and drill 3⁄32" (2.5mm)-diameter pilot holes in the corners. Then, use a #5 Flying Dutchman Polar blade to cut the perimeter of the acrylic lid. Use a slow cutting speed to keep the acrylic from melting back together. Remove the pattern and use a piece of tape to transfer the alignment mark to the acrylic.

14 **Drill the pilot holes in the lid.** Insert a 5⁄64" (2mm)-diameter bit in a drill press. Place the acrylic lid on top of the maze and set the drill press to drill a ½" (13mm)-deep hole. If you use a hand drill, wrap a piece of masking tape around the bit ½" (13mm) from the end. Then, drill through the holes in the acrylic into the wooden lid. Use a #2 by ½" (13mm)-long round-head brass screw to hold the acrylic in place while you drill another hole and insert another screw. Then, drill the remaining holes and remove the screws and acrylic.

15 **Complete the box.** Vacuum any particles from the maze area of the lid. Place five 5mm-diameter ball bearings into the maze. Remove the protective film from the acrylic piece and screw it into place with the four brass screws.

Maze-Lid Box Patterns

Further Reading

Creative Wooden Boxes from the Scroll Saw

By Carole Rothman

Searching for unique and interesting box projects for the scroll saw? Author Carole Rothman has created 28 beautiful designs for boxes you'll love to make and love to use. All of the projects are useful, surprisingly easy to make, and are great for gift giving.

Available for $24.95 plus S&H from Fox Chapel Publishing, 800-457-9112, foxchapelpublishing.com, or check your local retailer.

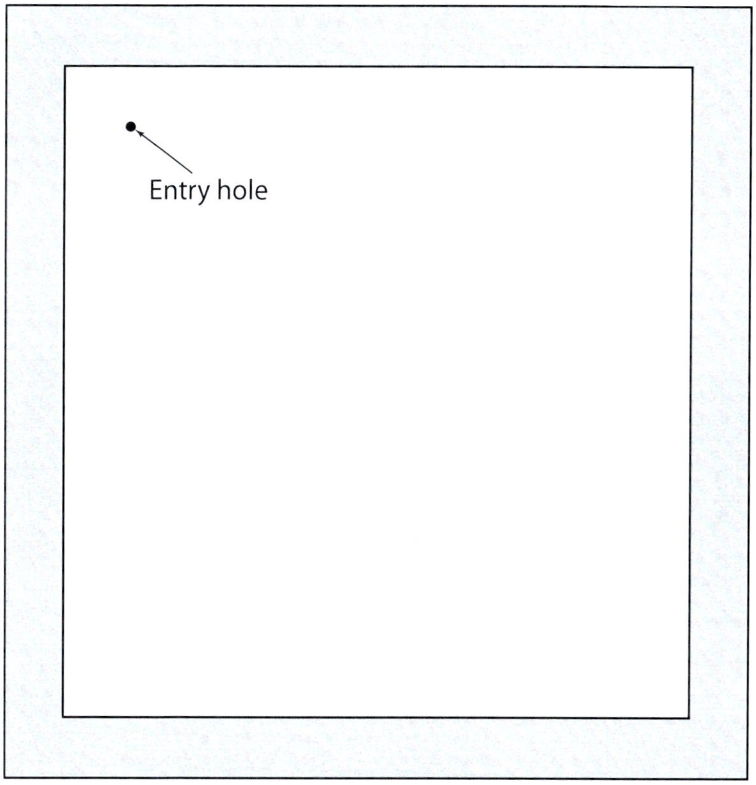

Materials & Tools

Materials

- Cherry, ¾" (1.9cm)-thick: box body, 4½" x 4½" (11.4cm x 11.4cm)
- Cherry, ¼" (6mm)-thick: maze, lid bottom, box bottom, 3 each 4½" x 4½" (11.4cm x 11.4cm)
- Cherry, ⅛" (3mm)-thick: lid liner, 4" x 4" (10.2cm x 10.2cm)
- Bloodwood, ⅛" (4mm)-thick: lid middle, 4½" x 4½" (11.4cm x 11.4cm)
- Clear acrylic plastic, ⅛" (3mm)-thick: 4½" x 4½" (11.4cm x 11.4cm)
- Repositionable adhesive
- Wood glue
- Sandpaper: assorted grits to 320
- Steel wool: 0000
- Lacquer: clear spray
- Packaging tape: clear
- Brass screws: 4 each #2 x ½" (13mm)
- Ball bearings: 5 each 5mm-diameter

Tools

- Blades, such as Flying Dutchman: #9, #3, #5 Polar
- Drill or drill press and bits: ¼" (6mm), 3/32" (2.5mm), 5/64" (2mm) diameters
- Awl
- Press or clamps
- Sanders

The author used these products for the project. Substitute your choice of brands, tools, and materials as desired.

Tiered Cake Box

Celebrate a special occasion with a gorgeous wooden cake

By Carole Rothman

Everyone loves beautiful cakes. This festive wooden version is also a two-tiered jewelry box with matching flocked interiors. This would be a great gift for friends, family, or that special someone—with or without something sparkly inside.

Much like my gift boxes in *Scroll Saw Woodworking & Crafts* Holiday 2014, this box uses compound cutting and lamination to make boxes with ribbons. But unlike the previous projects, this box needs icing! I added piped dots using MUD texturing compound, which looks like icing but dries hard, like wood. However, the texture of the compound is different from icing, so I highly recommend you practice on scrap wood before you tackle the cake. If you're looking for more of a challenge, I have added instructions for piping borders and other decorations.

Getting Started

Cut the blanks to size. Photocopy the patterns. You need one copy each of the top layer pattern, the bottom layer pattern, and the top tail pattern. You need four copies of the side tail pattern, 10 copies of the top loop pattern, and 24 copies of the side loop pattern. For the cake plate top pattern, either copy the halves and tape them together, or copy the pattern on larger paper.

MAKING THE LOOPS AND TAILS

1 **G**lue up the three laminated blanks. Use the lamination diagrams (at right). For ease in handling, start with the ¼" (6mm)-thick center blank and glue the veneer and thin wood blanks alternately to each side, in the order indicated, until all pieces are firmly attached. Clamp the laminated blanks and let them dry fully. Sand one long-grain edge of each lamination smooth. To prevent warping, keep the laminated blanks in a press until right before you cut them.

Lamination 1 - *ribbons on bottom layer*

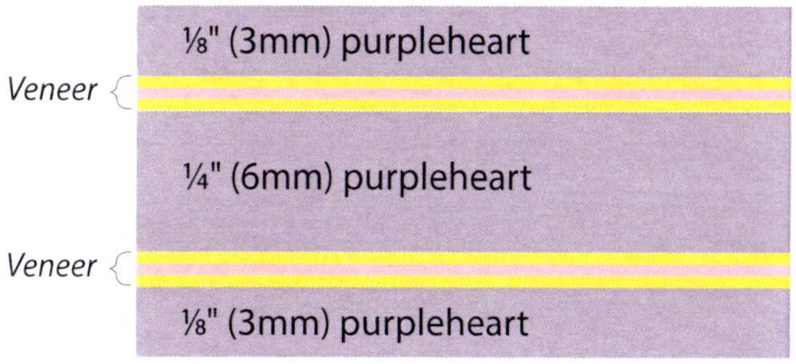

Lamination 2 - *ribbons on top layer*

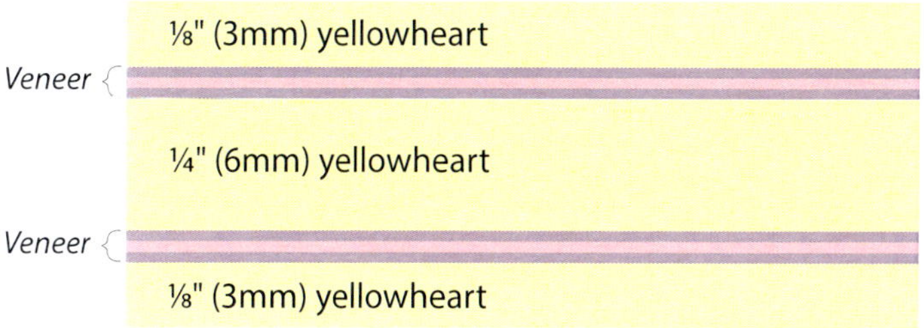

2 **Attach the side loop patterns.** Start at the sanded edge of lamination 1 and cut two ¾" by 6½" (1.9cm by 16.5cm) strips. Using repositionable adhesive, attach six side loop patterns to each strip. Center the face (solid) pattern between the stripes on the striped side, and the pattern with the drill hole marked on the plain side. Save the remainder of lamination 1 for the tails.

Lamination 3 - *ribbons on top of cake*

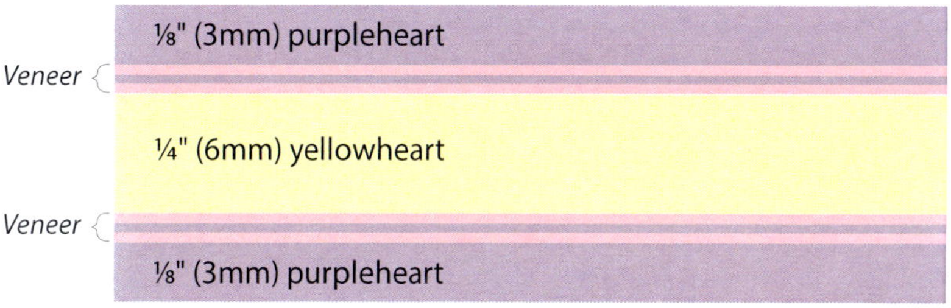

3 **Cut the sides of the loops.** Cover the drilled side with clear tape to avoid shredding the pattern. Drill where indicated with a 5⁄16" (8mm)-diameter bit, using a backer board to prevent tear out. Insert a blade and cut the inside of each loop. Then, cut the outside of each loop to free it from the blank. Replace each loop and tape it securely in place.

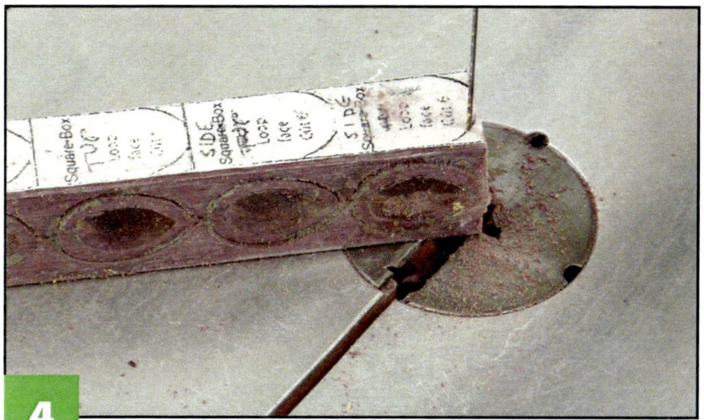

4 **Complete the loops.** Rotate the blank so the face side of the pattern is up. Cut along the curved bottom for the first loop. Remove the loop from the blank, cut off the waste, and repeat the process on the next loop. Repeat Steps 2 to 4 with lamination 2.

5 **Cut the loops for the top of the cake.** Cut two ¾" by 6" (1.9cm by 15.2cm) strips and one ¾" by 3" (1.9cm by 7.6cm) strip from lamination 3. Follow Steps 2 to 4 to attach patterns and cut four loops from each of the longer strips and two loops from the shorter strip. This will give you nine loops, plus one extra. Save the remainder of lamination 3 for the tails. Sand the inside and outside of the top and side loops until smooth.

TIP

SANDING THE LOOPS TO SHAPE

Instead of cutting the lower curve of the loops, you can shape them by sanding. Cut the loops as explained in Step 3, but do not tape them back in place. Skip Step 4. Use a belt sander to sand the outside of each loop smooth, and then sand the lower curve, referring to the pattern for shape.

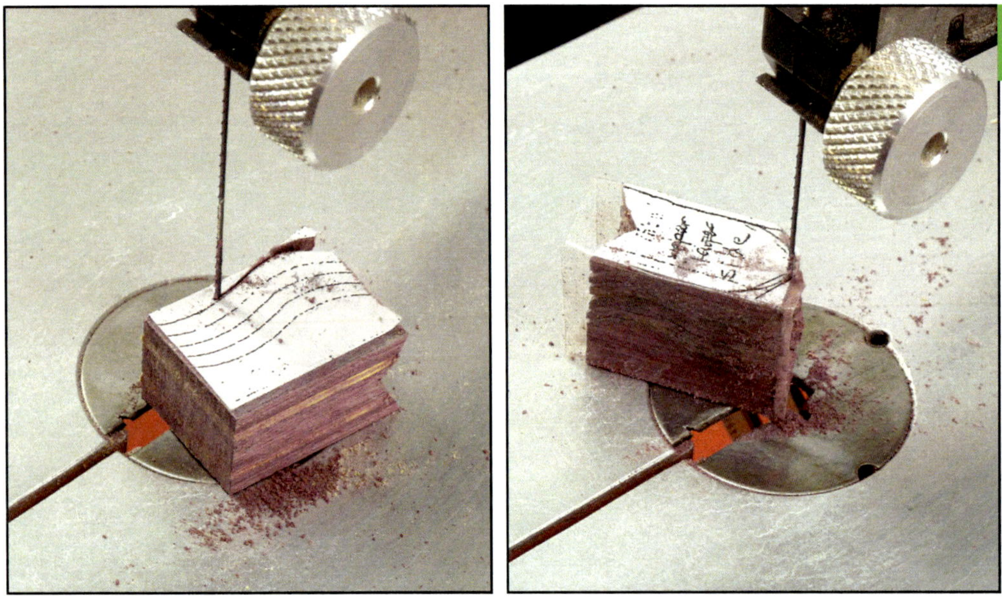

6 **Cut the side tails.** Cut two 1" by 1⅜" (2.5cm by 3.5cm) strips from lamination 1. Attach the face part of the pattern to the striped side of each strip, with the V centered between the stripes, and attach the side part of the pattern to the plain side. Place each strip face-side up and cut the top V. Rotate the blank 90° and cut along each line on the side pattern to form four tails. Use clear tape to reattach the tails and waste. Turn each strip face-side up and cut the lower curved edge to complete the tails. This will give you eight tails total. Repeat this process with lamination 2.

TIP

TESTING THE FIT OF THE RIBBONS

Use small loops of masking tape to secure the loops and tails to scrap wood to test their fit and position. Sand the contours so the pieces mate together tightly for gluing. Since many pieces have more than one gluing area, use these mock-ups to determine which area(s) should be masked before pre-finishing each piece.

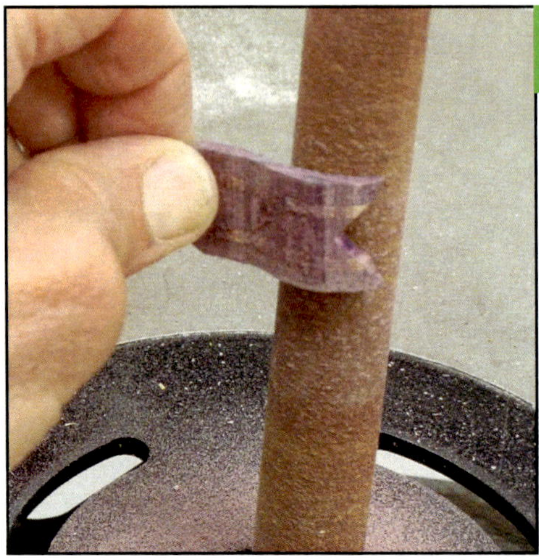

7 **Cut the top tails.** Cut one 1" by 2¼" (2.5cm by 7cm) strips from lamination 3 and repeat Step 6 to cut four tails (one tail is an extra). Sand the top and side tails until smooth.

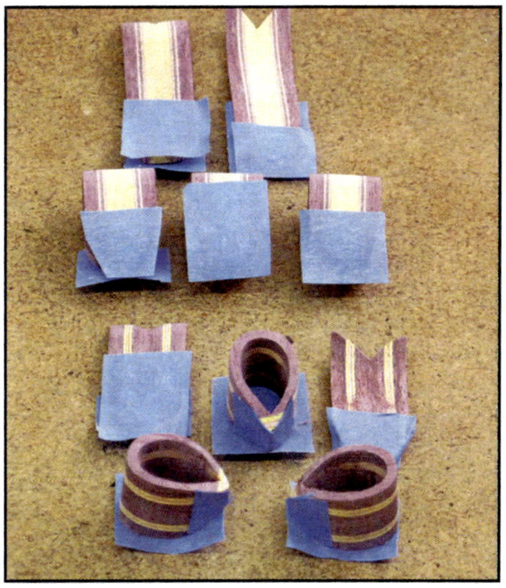

8 **Pre-finish the loops and tails.** Pre-finishing the loops and tails makes the finishing process in Step 25 easier. Apply blue painter's tape to the gluing surfaces on the loops and tails. Spray the unmasked areas with shellac and allow it to dry. Remove the tape, and buff each piece with a 320-grit sanding mop or hand-sand with 320-grit sandpaper.

MAKING THE CAKE PLATE

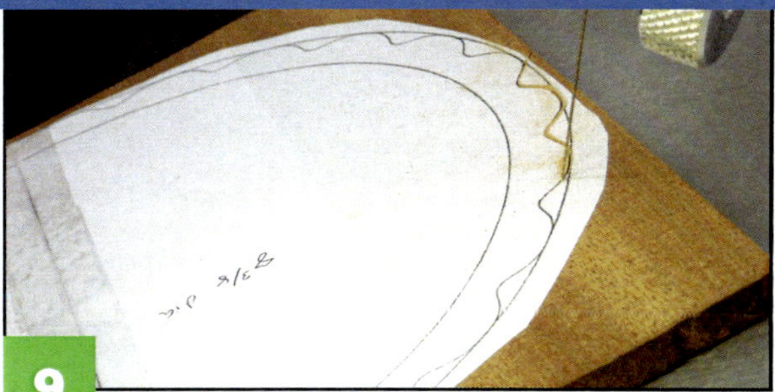

9 **Cut the top of the cake plate.** Attach the cake plate top pattern to the blank with repositionable adhesive. Tilt the left side of the saw table down to 30° and cut clockwise around the plate. Sand until smooth, and soften (round) the sharp edges. Use a spindle sander or sandpaper wrapped around a dowel.

10 **Cut the base pieces of the cake plate.** Use a compass to draw a 4" (10.2cm)-diameter circle on the blank. With the saw table still tilted down 30°, cut in a clockwise direction around the circle. Trace the outline of the smaller face of the just-cut piece onto the other base blank (it will have approximately a 3", or 7.6cm, diameter). Level the saw table and cut the circle.

11 **Finish the base pieces.** Glue and clamp the two base pieces together and let the glue dry. Use a spindle sander to sand a curve where the two pieces meet. Check your work frequently to keep the shaping even.

12 **Assemble the base.** Mark the center on the bottom side of the cake plate top, and use a compass to draw a circle slightly larger than the top of the base pieces. Use the circle as a guide to glue and clamp the base to the cake plate top.

MAKING THE LAYERS

13 **Cut the bottom layer.** Cover the blank with clear packaging tape and attach the pattern. Drill 1/16" (2mm)-diameter blade-entry holes where indicated. Thread the blade through the innermost hole and cut the circle to remove the center. Set aside the center to use for the top layer and its lid. Insert the blade into the other hole and cut around the circle to free the bottom layer. Remove it from the blank and sand the inside and the outside of the layer until smooth.

14 **Assemble the bottom lid.** Remove the pattern from the blank, but do not discard it. Sand the inside of the bottom lid until smooth. Remove any fuzzies from the bottom edge. Glue the lid to the bottom lid blank. Clamp the lid blank in place, allow it to set for a few minutes, unclamp, and remove any squeeze-out from inside the circle. Reclamp and let dry.

15 **Complete the bottom lid.** Reattach the pattern removed in Step 14, and cut along the outer circle. Sand until the outside is smooth and free of blade and scratch marks. Soften the upper edge.

16 **Make the top layer.** Repeat Steps 13 to 15 to cut the top layer and lid, using the center saved from Step 13, the top lid blank, and the top layer pattern.

ASSEMBLING THE PROJECT

17 **Attach the layers.** To guide the placement of the bottom layer, lightly draw a reference circle in the center of the cake plate. Center the bottom layer on the plate and glue it in place. Clamp firmly until dry. Draw a reference circle in the center of the bottom lid, and glue the top layer in place. Clamp firmly until dry.

18 **Mask the gluing areas for the ribbons.** Position the loops and tails for each lid in four evenly spaced clusters. The ribbons on the bottom layer should fall between those on the top layer. Position the ribbons for the top of the cake in the center. Mask all gluing areas with blue painter's tape.

19 **Seal the pieces.** Seal the inner and outer box surfaces with a coat of shellac. When the shellac dries, remove the tape and sand the sealed and unsealed surfaces with 320-grit sandpaper until smooth. Remove the dust.

ADDING THE DETAILS

20 **Mark the locations of the decorative dots (optional).** Although the dots add a festive look, you can omit them and still have an attractive project. To prepare the surface for piping, use a ruler and light pencil marks to create evenly spaced patterns of dots in the areas between the ribbon clusters. Pipe the dots individually or in small groups. Erase all previously drawn pencil marks, except for the small dots that will guide the piping.

21 **Pipe the decorative dots.** Place the bottom layer lid over a wide jar with the top layer lid in position. Put the assembly on a stable raised platform so you can work more easily. If you are using a coupler, trim the end of a disposable plastic piping bag and insert the body of the coupler so the threads protrude. Place a #1 tip into the ring of the coupler, and screw the ring and tip to the body of the coupler. If you are not using a coupler, trim the end of a plastic or parchment bag and drop a #1 tip into the bag. Fill the bag with a small amount of MUD, and pipe small dots where marked in Step 20. Remove any misplaced or misshapen dots immediately with a damp brush, clean away the residue, and re-pipe. Let the dots set until firm. Clean all tools with water, soaking them if needed to remove dried MUD.

22 **Prepare the lids for the side loops and tails.** Divide the loops and tails from each lamination into four clusters, each consisting of two tails and three loops. For each cluster, glue two of the loops to the tails, using a toothpick to apply wood glue, such as Nexabond, to the sides of the loops and pressing the tails into place. On each lid, lightly mark the center of each cluster location at the top of the lid. Draw a line down the side at that point. Put the top lid in place and make sure the ribbon clusters of the top lid will be aligned with the dot clusters on the bottom lid.

FINISHING THE PROJECT

23 **Attach the loops and tails to the bottom and top layers.** Use masking tape to hold a sample loop in place on one of the layers. Slide the matching loops and tails into position under it. The bottom of the cluster can sit flush with the bottom edge of the lid or just above it. Mark the top of the loop. Measure the distance from the top of the layer to this mark, and mark that distance with a small dot at each of the eight gluing locations. Remove all other pencil marks. At each location, use Nexabond glue to lock the top loop into place, holding it until set. Let it dry fully. Check the matching tail assemblies for fit, and sand the lower edge or underside of the tails if needed. Glue the assemblies into place, holding firmly until set.

> **TIP**
> **EASY GLUING**
> *If you have a vise with non-marring jaws, clamp the lid in a horizontal position for ease in gluing and drying the bow clusters.*

24 **Attach the loops and tails to the top of the cake.** Separate the six loops for the lower layer of the ribbon cluster from the three loops for the upper layer. Glue the tails to the upper loops. Use small loops of masking tape to position the six lower loops in a circle at the center of the lid. Test the fit of the loop-tail assemblies and adjust the lower loops as needed. Glue on the six lower loops, one at a time, holding until set. Glue the three tail-loop assemblies in place and hold until set. Let the pieces dry thoroughly.

25 **Apply a clear lacquer finish.** Sand away any glue residue on the ribbon clusters and box surfaces. Apply several coats of glossy spray lacquer to the lids and cake stand. Do not spray the box interiors or the insides of the lids.

26 **Flock the box interiors.** Apply a generous coat of acrylic paint that matches the flocking fibers to the inside of the box. Spray or pour a large amount of flocking fibers, and let the paint dry overnight. Then, tap out the excess fiber for reuse.

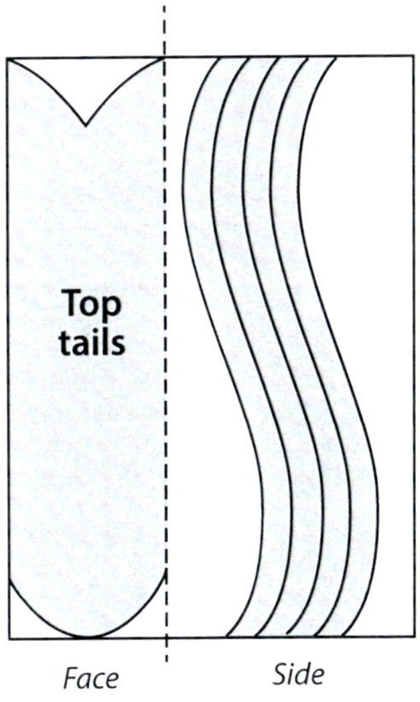

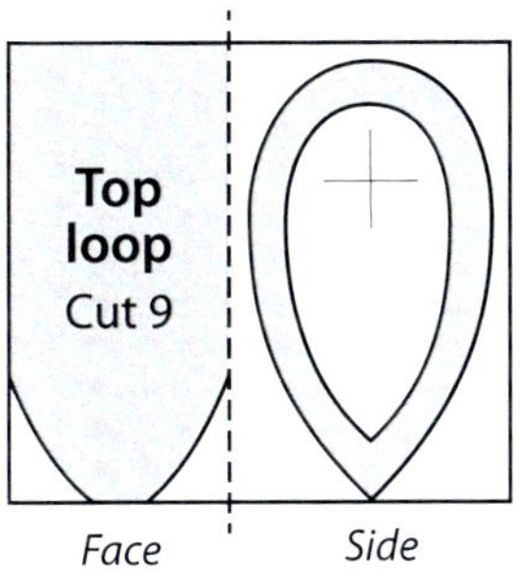

Cake Box Patterns

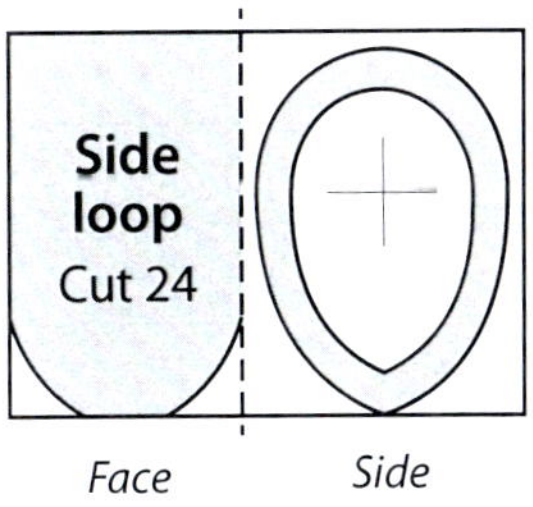

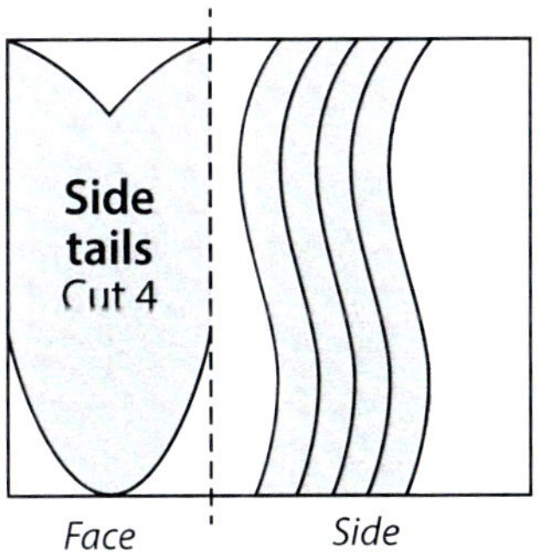

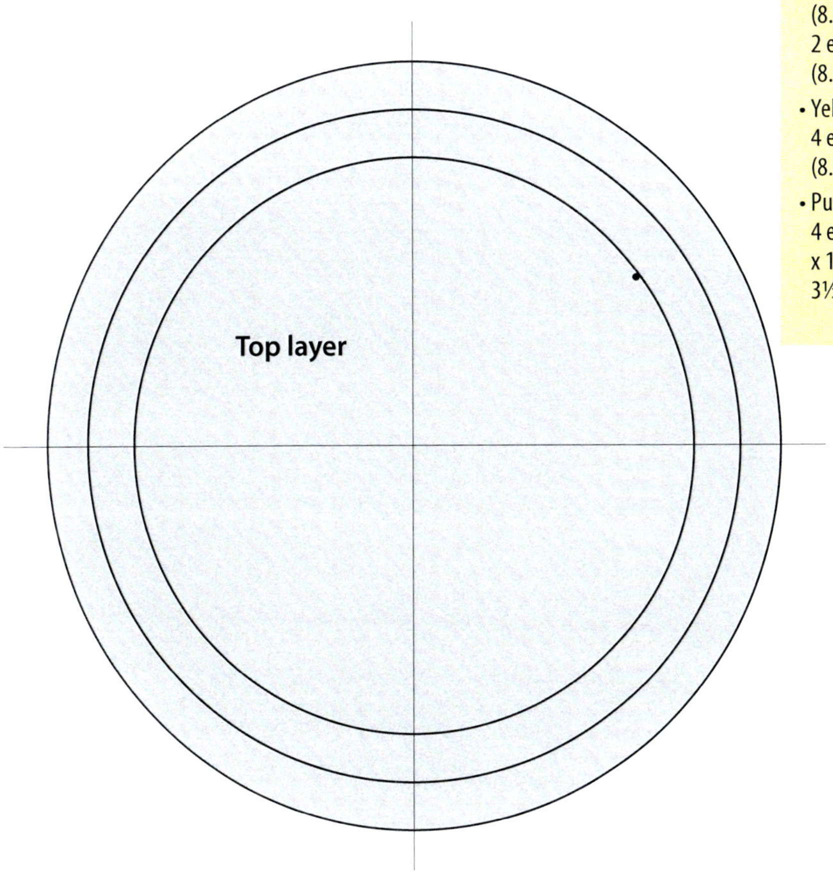

Materials & Tools

Materials

- Maple, 1⅜" (3.5cm) thick: top and bottom layers and lids, 7" x 7" (17.8cm x 17.8cm)
- Maple, ⅛" (3mm) thick: bottom lid, 7" x 7" (17.8cm x 17.8cm); top lid, 5" x 5" (12.7cm x 12.7cm)

Wood for the cake plate

- Sapele, ¾" (1.9cm) thick: cake plate base bottom, 4½" x 4½" (22.9cm x 22.9cm); cake plate base middle, 4" x 4" (10.2cm x 10.2cm)
- Sapele, ¼" (6mm) thick: cake plate top, 9" x 9" (22.9cm x 22.9cm)

Wood for lamination blocks

- Yellowheart, ¼" (6mm) thick: lamination 2, 3½" x 6½" (8.9cm x 16.5cm); lamination 3, 3½" x 6" (8.9cm x 15.2cm)
- Yellowheart, ⅛" (3mm) thick: lamination 2, 2 each 3½" x 6½" (8.9cm x 16.5cm)
- Purpleheart, ¼" (6mm) thick: lamination 1, 3½" x 6½" (8.9cm x 16.5cm)
- Purpleheart, ⅛" (3mm) thick: lamination 1, 2 each 3½" x 6½" (8.9cm x 16.5cm); lamination 3, 2 each 3½" x 6" (8.9cm x 15.2cm)
- Yellow veneer: lamination 1, 4 each 3½" x 6½" (8.9cm x 16.5cm)
- Purple veneer: lamination 2, 4 each 3½" x 6½" (8.9cm x 16.5cm); lamination 3, 2 each 3½" x 6" (8.9cm x 15.2cm)
- Pink veneer: lamination 1, 2 each 3½" x 6½" (8.9cm x 16.5cm); lamination 2, 2 each 3½" x 6½" (8.9cm x 16.5cm); lamination 3, 4 each 3½" x 6" (8.9cm x 15.2cm)
- Spray adhesive: repositionable
- Glue: wood, such as Weldbond; Nexabond (for loops)
- Sandpaper
- MUD texturing compound (see Special Sources) (optional)
- Tape: blue painter's and clear packing
- Spray shellac
- Spray lacquer
- Acrylic paint and matching flocking fibers

Tools

- Blades: #5 skip tooth, such as Flying Dutchman Polar
- Compass
- Drill with bits: 5/16" (8mm), 1/16 (2mm) dia.
- Press or clamps and boards
- Sanders: assorted types
- Disposable piping bag (plastic or parchment) (optional)
- Piping coupler (optional)
- Piping tip #1 (optional)

The author used these products for the project. Substitute your choice of brands, tools, and materials as desired.

SPECIAL SOURCES

MUD texturing compound is available from Margot Clark at margotclark.com.

Print x2 and connect the pieces in the center to make the full board top.

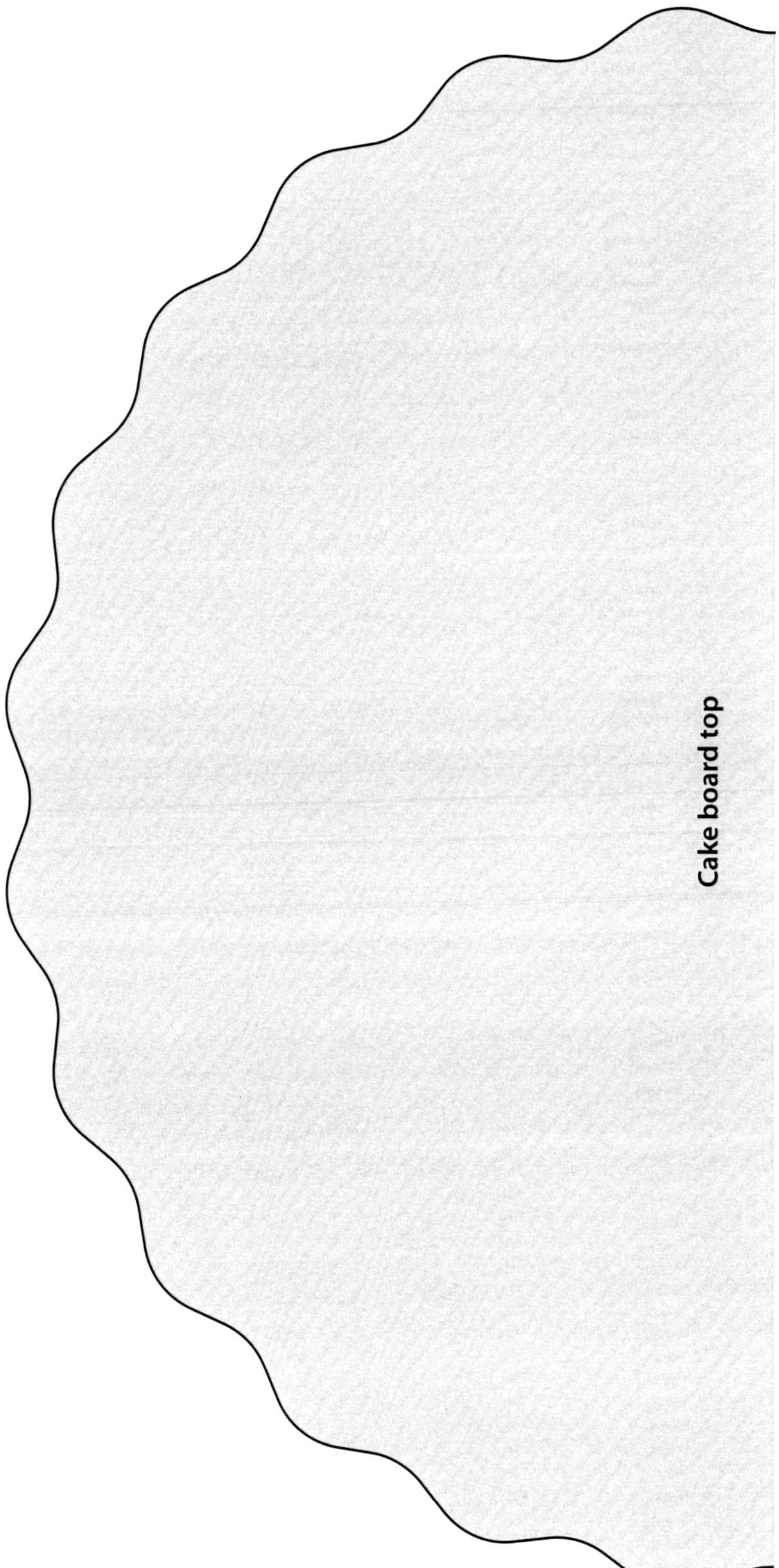

Cake Box Patterns

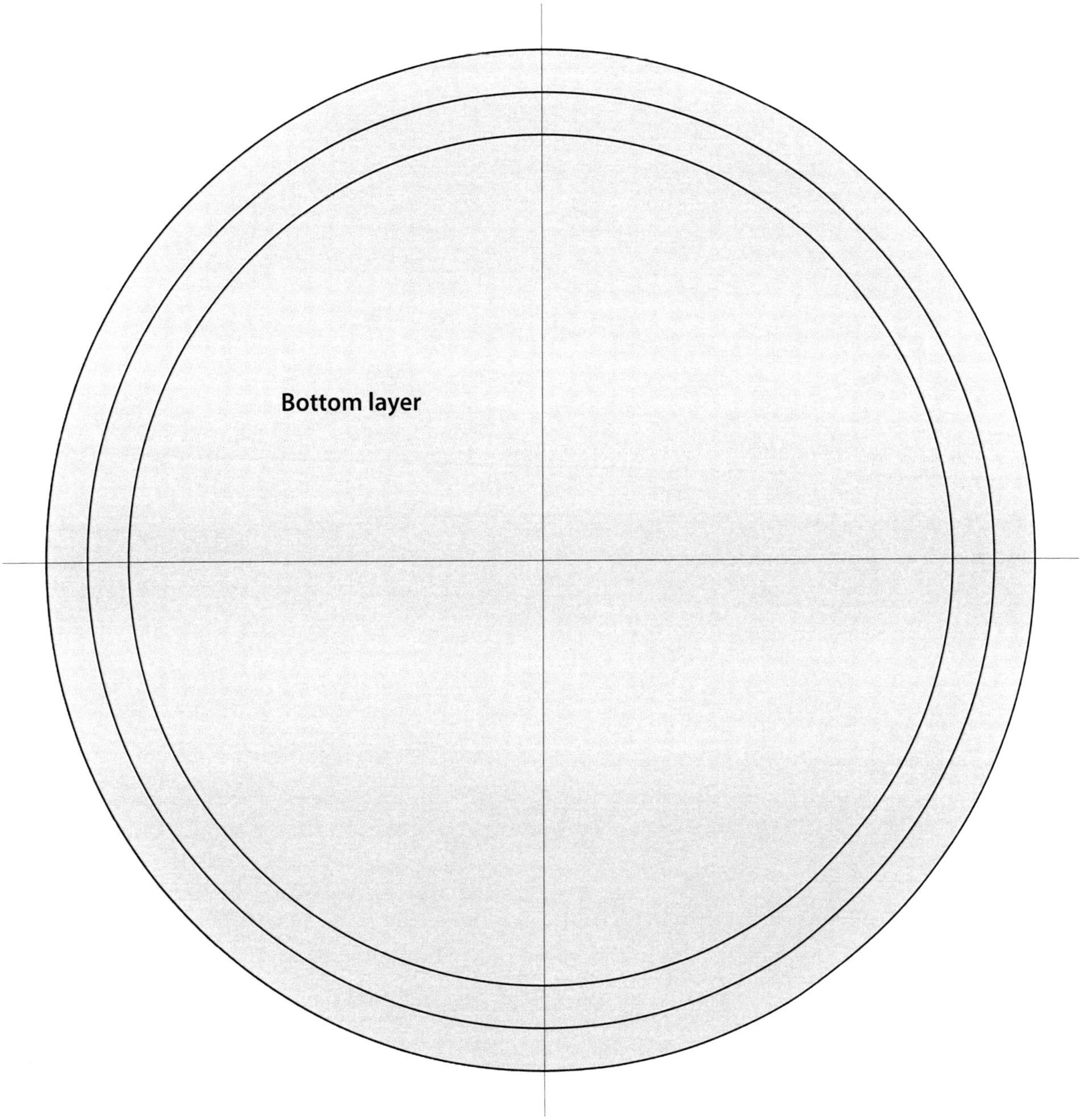

Hamsa Box

Combine colorful veneer and hardwoods to make a meaningful gift

By Carole Rothman

The hand-shaped hamsa symbol is believed to bring luck, good health, and protection from the forces of evil. It has a special place in Judaism and is also a sacred and respected symbol in Christianity, Islam, Hinduism, and Buddhism.

Although the hamsa is usually worn as a pendant, I incorporated it into a box for a friend down on her luck. I used brightly colored veneer to symbolize my wishes for happier days ahead and was pleased when my gift was received in the spirit intended.

VENEERING THE LID

1 **Position one piece of red veneer with the grain running vertically.** On each long side, make a small pencil mark 2" (5.1cm) up from the bottom edge. Place the red veneer on a larger piece of thin cardboard, matching the edges. Place the strips of yellow and purple veneer across the red veneer with their lower edges at the 2" (5.1cm) mark. Attach these strips at the short ends to the red veneer and cardboard using masking tape.

2 **Cut along the two horizontal dotted lines of the lid pattern to access the eye pattern.** Using a glue stick, attach the pattern to the smaller piece of cardboard. Place the pattern and cardboard, top edge up, across the purple and yellow veneer, and secure it with masking tape at the top, side, and bottom edges.

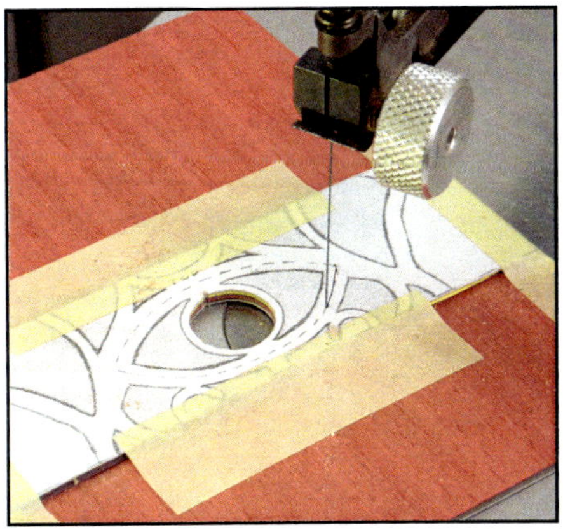

3 **Drill a small blade-entry hole on the dotted cutting line of the circle.** Insert a #2/0 blade through the hole and cut around the circle. Carefully remove the pieces. Repeat for the eye-shaped dotted cutting line. Separate all of the pieces and place the eye-shaped yellow piece and the round purple piece into position on the red veneer. The remaining pieces of veneer can be used for another project.

COMPLETING THE LID

4 **Tape the eye pieces into position on the red veneer.** Use veneer tape or masking tape on the upper surfaces. Glue this assembly to the top face of the lid and glue the remaining piece of red veneer to the bottom face. Use a veneer roller on each side to get a good bond. Clamp the pieces securely and let the assembly dry. Carefully remove the tape from the eye area. Sand the surfaces carefully to even the grain, removing sanding dust with a vacuum or damp paper towel. Be careful to keep red veneer dust off the yellow veneer.

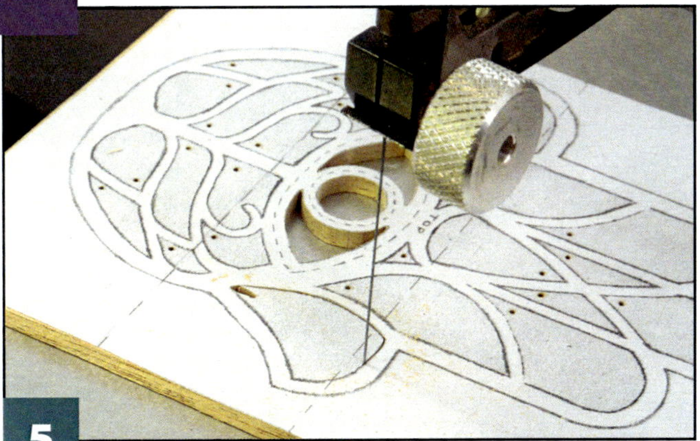

5 **Attach the lid pattern to the top fretwork blank.** Use repositionable adhesive. Drill blade-entry holes in the internal areas and cut the frets using a #1 blade. Remove the internal parts of the pattern (on the bridges between the frets) so you can see and correct any irregularities and blade marks, but keep the perimeter of the pattern intact. Carefully sand the exposed fretwork bridges smooth.

6 **Glue the fretwork to the veneered lid.** Make sure the joints between the pieces of veneer are covered by the fretwork. To minimize squeeze-out, apply glue only to the wider areas of the perimeter and eye. Clamp and let it dry for five minutes. Remove the clamps and carefully remove any squeeze-out, re-clamp, and let dry fully. Cut along the perimeter of the lid pattern with a #3 blade, cutting to the outside of the line.

MAKING THE BODY

7 **Attach the box body pattern to the body blank.** Mark the drilling points for the dowels with an awl. Drill a blade-entry hole where indicated and cut the box interior with a #7 blade. Do not remove the pattern. Sand the inside smooth using a spindle sander. Remove any fuzzies from the lower edge.

8 **Glue the bottom to the underside of the box body.** Clamp, let dry five minutes, and then remove the clamps to remove any squeeze-out. Re-clamp and let dry fully. Cut around the perimeter with a #7 blade, cutting to the outside of the line. Remove the pattern.

TIP

DRILLING DEPTH

If you are using a drill press, mark the box body and lid at the desired depths. For each piece, adjust the depth of the hole as instructed. If you are using a hand drill, mark the drilling depth with a piece of tape on the drill bit.

COMPLETING THE PROJECT

9 **Drill holes for the lid dowels in the box body.** Use a ¼" (6mm)-diameter bit to drill two ½" (1.3cm)-deep holes where marked on the box body. Insert a ¼" (6mm) dowel center into each hole. Place the lid on top, carefully aligning it with the box body. Press down gently on the lid to mark the drilling points in the lid. Use the same bit to drill 3⁄16" (5mm)-deep holes at the marked points, being careful not to drill through the lid.

10 **Insert the dowel pieces into the holes in the base.** Sand them until they fit easily but snugly. Round the top edges of the dowels and place the lid on top to check the fit. Adjust the length of the dowels until the lid sits flat on the box body. Remove the dowels, apply a light coat of glue, and seat them into the holes in the body using a wooden mallet if needed.

11 **Place the lid on the box body.** Sand the completed box as one piece until the sides are smooth and the lid and box body are evenly matched. You can use a belt sander for the rounded lower edge and a spindle sander for the curved areas. Use a sanding block for the hard-to-reach areas, and soften the upper edges by hand. Sand all of the surfaces up to 220 grit. Remove all of the sanding dust, using a vacuum for the recessed areas. Finish with several coats of spray shellac or lacquer, rubbing between coats with 0000 steel wool as needed.

Materials & Tools

Materials

- Mahogany, 1⅛" (29mm) thick: box body, 5½" x 7" (140mm x 178mm)
- Mahogany, 5⁄16" (8mm) thick: lid, 5½" x 7" (140mm x 178mm)
- Mahogany, ⅛" (3mm) thick: box bottom, 5½" x 7" (140mm x 178mm)
- Mahogany, 3⁄16" (5mm) thick: lid fretwork, 5½" x 7" (140mm x 178mm)
- Red veneer: 2 each, 5½" x 7" (140mm x 178mm)
- Yellow veneer: 1¾" x 5½" (44mm x 140mm)
- Purple veneer: 1¾" x 5½" (44mm x 140mm)
- Hardwood dowel, ¼" (6mm) dia.: 2 each, 11⁄16" (18mm) long
- Thin cardboard: 1¾" x 5½" (44mm x 140mm), 5½" x 7" (140mm x 178mm)
- Tape: masking, veneer (optional)
- Wood glue, Weldbond preferred
- Glue stick
- Repositionable adhesive
- Sandpaper, assorted grits
- Finish: spray shellac or spray lacquer
- Steel wool: 0000

Tools

- Drill press with bits: #60 wire size or smaller, ¼" (6mm) dia., brad point preferred
- Scroll saw blades, #2/0, #1, #3, #7
- Sanders: spindle, belt
- Awl
- Dowel centers: 2 each, ¼" (6mm) dia.
- Veneer roller
- Clamps
- Wooden mallet

The author used these products for the project. Substitute your choice of brands, tools, and materials as desired.

Hamsa Box Pattern

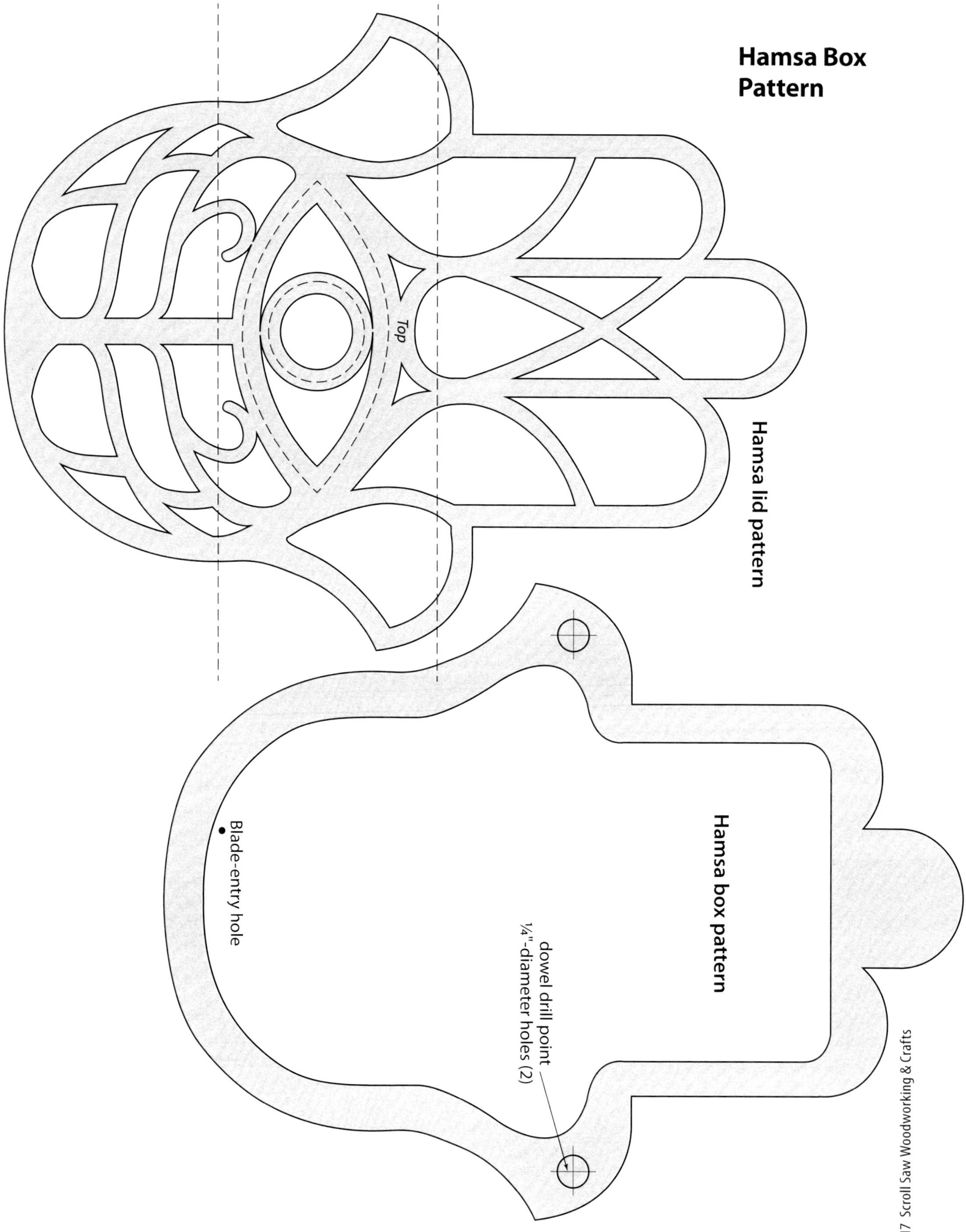

Christmas Rose Box

A compound-cut flower is the perfect accent for this unusual box design

By Carole Rothman

Flowers that bloom in winter are special, bringing surprising beauty during stark weather. This festive box, with its colorful ribbons and faithful rendition of the Christmas rose (Helleborus niger) will bring year-long cheer to the lucky recipient.

I sanded and shaped the compound-cut petals to achieve a delicate look. Two products familiar to cake decorators—artificial stamens and dusting powders—add a realistic touch to the completed flower. Narrow strips of dyed red veneer, cut across the grain, look exactly like grosgrain ribbon and are flexible enough to bend around gentle curves.

The box body is easy to make, with a round interior that makes sanding a snap. I cut the lid from thin wood to reduce stress on the petals, which serve as handles. To minimize the tendency of the lid to cup, the lid liner was made from thicker wood, cut and re-glued to increase stability.

Getting Started

Attach a copy of the pattern to the box body blank using repositionable adhesive. Drill a blade-entry hole just inside the largest circle. Then, attach a copy of the pattern to the blank for the box top and drill a blade-entry hole inside the smaller circle.

MAKING THE BOX

1 **Cut and sand the inside of the box body.** Use a #7 blade. Remove the center of the pattern and save it for Steps 7 and 8. Sand with a spindle sander.

2 **Glue and clamp the box bottom to the body.** Allow it to dry for 10 minutes, loosen the clamps, remove any squeeze-out, re-clamp, and let the glue dry fully. Cut the perimeter and remove the pattern. Use a belt sander to smooth the outside of the body. Check the length of each side to ensure all of them are equal; sand to adjust as needed.

3 **Make the box top.** Cut along the smallest circle with a #3 blade. Then, cut the perimeter of the top, cutting to the outside of the line. Use a spindle sander to sand the opening until it's smooth and regular.

4 **Seal the inside of the box.** Apply a coat of shellac to the inside of the box body and the underside of the box top. Do not apply shellac to the gluing surfaces. When the shellac is dry, sand the sealed surface lightly with 220-grit sandpaper.

5 **Glue and clamp the box top to the box body.** Keep the overlap even on all of the sides. After the glue is dry, sand the box top flush with the body, and make sure all eight sides are the same. Mark the center of each side on the underside of the box to help with the ribbon placement later.

6 **Bevel the box top.** Set the belt sander table to 45° and sand a bevel that extends ⅛" (3mm) down from the top. Use a pneumatic drum sander to shape the bevel into a soft curve. Use the drum sander to soften (round) the edges of the bottom, sides, and center opening. Hand-sand the exterior of the entire box with progressively finer grits of sandpaper up to 220 grit.

MAKING THE LID

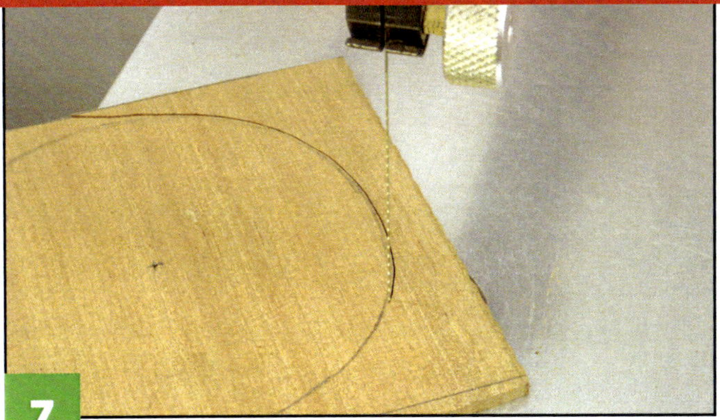

7 **Cut the lid.** Attach the remainder of the pattern saved from Step 1 to the lid blank, or draw a 4½" (114mm)-diameter circle on the blank. Mark the center point clearly with an awl. Cut to the outside of the line with a #3 blade. Remove the pattern and save for Step 8. Sand the edge of the lid until smooth. Use the pneumatic drum sander to round the upper edge of the lid into a smooth curve.

TIP

REDUCING WOOD MOVEMENT

Natural hardwoods can warp, cup, and twist based on the seasonal changes in humidity. Thin woods cup and twist easier than thicker woods. We will cut and re-glue the wood for the lid liner to increase its resistance to cupping. If you cut two 4½" (114mm) squares rather than one and exchange halves after the first glue-up, you'll end up with two lid-liner blanks, one with all endgrain at the edges and the other with all face grain, for a very attractive look. These glued joints aren't very strong, but they only need to hold until you cut the liner and glue it to the lid.

8 **Cut the lid liner blank in half on the diagonal.** Sand or joint the edges smooth. Invert one of the pieces and glue the two halves together. To get a good joint, rub the pieces back and forth until they drag and then let the assembly dry on waxed paper. Cut the glued blank in half again on the other diagonal and glue again. When the glue is dry, sand both sides smooth. Then, use the pattern saved from Step 7, or draw a 4" (102mm) circle with a compass, and cut the circle. Check the fit by holding the liner with a piece of masking tape, and then inserting the liner into the top opening. It should rotate freely. *Note: Before attaching the lid liner, choose the most attractive face of the box body for the front and mark it. Then, place the lid on the box, rotate it to find the best grain match, and mark the front of the lid.*

9 **Attach the lid liner to the lid.** Use masking tape to attach the lid liner to the lid. Insert the assembly into the box opening, making sure the fronts of the box and lid are aligned, and center the lid on the box top. Mark the position of the liner on the lid. Remove the liner and tape. Apply dots of Nexabond glue to the lid liner, press it into position, and let dry, clamping if needed.

ADDING THE RIBBONS

10 **Draw the guidelines for the ribbons.** Use a straight edge and square to divide the lid and box into quarters, using the center mark as a guide. Ensure the lines are vertical and centered on the box sides. Remove the lid. Extend the box lines into the opening and the lid lines to the under side.

11

Cut the veneer ribbons. Use a hobby knife, straight edge, and self-healing mat. For the lid, cut three ½" (1.3cm)-long by 5" (12.7cm)-wide strips of red veneer, cutting across the grain. For the box top and sides, cut eight ½" (1.3cm)-long by 4" (10.2cm)-wide strips. The extra strips allow for breakage.

TIP

TERMINOLOGY

To prevent miscuts when cutting the veneer ribbons, note that "length" is measured along the grain and "width" is measured across the grain.

12

Attach the first lid ribbon. Trim a 5" (12.7cm)-long strip so it extends slightly past the bottom edge of the lid when laid across the center. Apply a thin, even layer of wood glue to the part of the strip that attaches to the top of the lid; use Nexabond glue on the ends that curve around the edges of the lid. Position the center of the strip on the pencil marks. Press and hold the ends flush against the curved edges of the lid.

13

Attach the second lid ribbon. Mark the center of the glued strip with an awl, using the remaining pencil line as a guide. Cut a 5" (12.7cm)-long strip in half. Butt one end of each half against the glued ribbon and mark the other end where it meets the edge of the lid. Trim each strip so it extends slightly beyond the bottom edge and glue them into place as in Step 12. When the strips are dry, trim the overhanging veneer with a hobby knife and sand the edges to soften. Place the lid on the box in its proper orientation. Check the pencil lines on the box for continuity with the lid ribbons and redraw if necessary.

14

Attach the box ribbons. Elevate the box slightly to accommodate the veneer overhang. Trim four of the 4" (10.2cm)-long strips so they extend from the box opening to slightly below the lower edge, easing the strips gently over the edge of the box top to prevent breakage. For each strip, apply a thin coat of wood glue evenly over the surface. Using the top and bottom pencil marks as guides, start at the top opening and work downward carefully to the box bottom, pressing the strip firmly into place. Put the lid in place briefly to check for correct positioning of the ribbon. Remove any glue squeeze-out. Let the glue dry thoroughly.

15 **Finish the box.** When the glue is dry, trim away any veneer that protrudes into the top opening and trim the ends flush with the bottom of the box. Sand a slight bevel onto all of the ribbon edges to prevent snagging. Sand the faces of the strips up to 240 grit. Use blue painter's tape to mask the center of the lid where the petals will be glued. Apply a sealer coat of shellac to all accessible surfaces of the box and lid. Mark and sand away any glue spots. Remove the blue tape. Sand the box and lid smooth with 320-grit sandpaper.

ADDING THE FLOWER

16 **Cut the petals.** Clamp the blank between two pieces of scrap with the side-view pattern up. Cut the side profile with a #7 blade. Tape the pieces back together with clear packaging tape and cut the top profile. Remove the petal from the scrap. Repeat the process to cut six petals (the extra petal will allow for breakage).

17 **Sand the petals.** Use a 1½" (38mm) spindle sander to smooth the upper and lower curves. Carefully use a belt sander to remove irregularities on the edges and flat surfaces. Check the thickness of the edges as you sand for uniformity, sanding until the petal is about 3⁄32" (2.5mm) thick. Use a pneumatic drum to round the upper edges. This gives the petal a more delicate look without making it excessively fragile. Finish sanding by hand up to 240 grit.

18 **Dry-assemble the petals.** Mask the gluing surface of the petals with blue tape. Apply a sealer coat of shellac to the petals and let dry. Remove the tape and sand with 320-grit sandpaper. Using loops of masking tape, position the petals on the lid. Their bottom ends should meet at the awl mark in the center of the lid.

19 **Attach the petals.** Working one petal at a time, remove the petal and tape, apply Nexabond glue, return the petal to its position, and hold until the glue sets. Repeat with the remaining petals and let them dry fully.

20 **Color the center of the flower.** Use petal dust, powdered colors, or diluted acrylic paint to color the center 1" (2.5cm) of the flower. Use scraps of aspen to test your colors and concentration. The goal is to obtain a light wash of color. Apply several coats of spray lacquer to the box and lid. Rub down between coats with 0000 steel wool as needed. Apply the spray in thin coats to avoid drips and sags.

21 **Add the stamens.** Clamp the lid firmly to the drill press table and set the depth stop about ⅛" (3mm) above the table. Drill a ¼" (6mm)-diameter hole in the center of the flower. Gather enough stamens to fill the hole without forcing. Trim the ends so the stamens flare outward without sprawling excessively. If you'd like a contrasting center, use a single lily stamen, colored with paint or petal dust.

22 **Glue the stamens.** Fill the hole about halfway with Nexabond glue and push the stamens in firmly. Use a toothpick or tweezers to arrange them, and remove any stamens that bend or cannot be positioned properly. Add extra stamens if needed before the glue sets.

Rose Petal Pattern

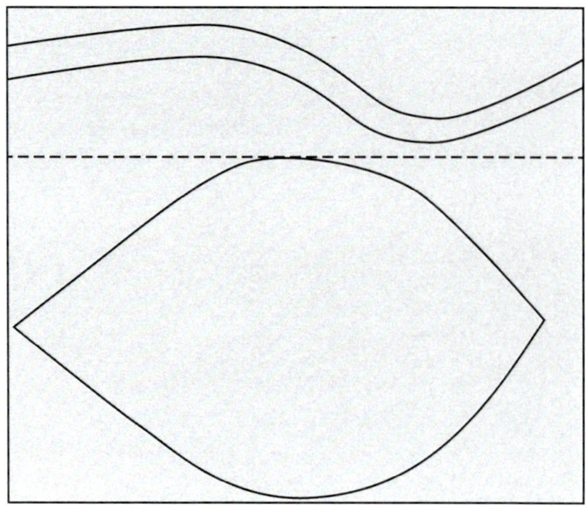